B

CW01456081

by Iain Gray

Lang**Syne**

PUBLISHING

WRITING *to* REMEMBER

Lang**Syne**

PUBLISHING

WRITING *to* REMEMBER

79 Main Street, Newtongrange,
Midlothian EH22 4NA
Tel: 0131 344 0414
E-mail: info@lang-syne.co.uk
www.langsyneshop.co.uk

Design by Dorothy Meikle
Printed by Printwell Ltd
© Lang Syne Publishers Ltd 2024

ISBN 978-1-85217-756-0

Burnett

MOTTO:
Courage flourishes at a wound

CREST:
A hand with a knife
pruning a vine tree

TERRITORIES include:
Aberdeenshire, the Borders,
Fife, Midlothian

NAME variations include:
Bernard
Burnat
Burnatt
Burnet
Burnette

Chapter one:

The origins of popular surnames

by George Forbes and Iain Gray

If you don't know where you came from, you won't know where you're going is a frequently quoted observation and one that has a particular resonance today when there has been a marked upsurge in interest in genealogy, with increasing numbers of people curious to trace their family roots.

Main sources for genealogical research include census returns and official records of births, marriages and deaths – and the key to unlocking the detail they contain is obviously a family surname, one that has been 'inherited' and passed from generation to generation.

No matter our station in life, we all have a surname – but it was not until about the middle of the fourteenth century that the practice of being identified by a particular surname became commonly established throughout the British Isles.

Previous to this, it was normal for a person to be identified through the use of only a forename.

But as population gradually increased and there were many more people with the same forename, surnames were adopted to distinguish one person, or community, from another.

Many common English surnames are patronymic in origin, meaning they stem from the forename of one's father – with 'Johnson,' for example, indicating 'son of John.'

It was the Normans, in the wake of their eleventh century conquest of Anglo-Saxon England, a pivotal moment in the nation's history, who first brought surnames into usage – although it was a gradual process.

For the Normans, these were names initially based on the title of their estates, local villages and chateaux in France to distinguish and identify these landholdings.

Such grand descriptions also helped enhance the prestige of these warlords and generally glorify their lofty positions high above the humble serfs slaving away below in the pecking order who had only single names, often with Biblical connotations as in Pierre and Jacques.

The only descriptive distinctions among the peasantry concerned their occupations, like 'Pierre the swineherd' or 'Jacques the ferryman.'

Roots of surnames that came into usage in England not only included Norman-French, but also Old French, Old Norse, Old English, Middle English, German, Latin, Greek, Hebrew and the Gaelic languages of the Celts.

The Normans themselves were originally Vikings, or 'Northmen', who raided, colonised and eventually settled down around the French coastline.

They had sailed up the Seine in their long-boats in 900AD under their ferocious leader Rollo and ruled the roost in north eastern France before sailing over to conquer England in 1066 under Duke William of Normandy – better known to posterity as William the Conqueror, or King William I of England.

Granted lands in the newly-conquered England, some of their descendants later acquired territories in Wales, Scotland and Ireland – taking not only their own surnames, but also the practice of adopting a surname, with them.

But it was in England where Norman rule and custom first impacted, particularly in relation to the adoption of surnames.

This is reflected in the famous *Domesday Book*, a massive survey of much of England and Wales, ordered by William I, to determine who owned what, what it was worth and therefore how much they were liable to pay in taxes to the voracious Royal Exchequer.

Completed in 1086 and now held in the National Archives in Kew, London, 'Domesday' was an Old English word meaning 'Day of Judgement.'

This was because, in the words of one contemporary chronicler, "its decisions, like those of the Last Judgement, are unalterable."

It had been a requirement of all those English landholders – from the richest to the poorest – that they identify themselves for the purposes of the survey and for future reference by means of a surname.

This is why the *Domesday Book*, although written in Latin as was the practice for several centuries with both civic and ecclesiastical records, is an invaluable source for the early appearance of a wide range of English surnames.

Several of these names were coined in connection with occupations.

These include Baker and Smith, while Cooks, Chamberlains, Constables and Porters were to be found carrying out duties in large medieval households.

The church's influence can be found in names such as Bishop, Friar and Monk while the popular name of Bennett derives from the late fifth to mid-sixth century Saint Benedict, founder of the Benedictine order of monks.

The early medical profession is represented by Barber, while businessmen produced names that include Merchant and Sellers.

Down at the village watermill, the names that cropped up included Millar/Miller, Walker and Fuller, while other self-explanatory trades included Cooper, Tailor, Mason and Wright.

Even the scenery was utilised as in Moor, Hill, Wood and Forrest – while the hunt and the chase supplied names that include Hunter, Falconer, Fowler and Fox.

Colours are also a source of popular surnames, as in Black, Brown, Gray/Grey, Green and White, and would have denoted the colour of the clothing the person habitually wore or, apart from the obvious exception of 'Green', one's hair colouring or even complexion.

The surname Red developed into Reid, while

Blue was rare and no-one wanted to be associated with yellow.

Rather self-important individuals took surnames that include Goodman and Wiseman, while physical attributes crept into surnames such as Small and Little.

Many families proudly boast the heraldic device known as a Coat of Arms, as featured on our front cover.

The central motif of the Coat of Arms would originally have been what was sometimes borne on the shield of a warrior to distinguish himself from others on the battlefield.

Not featured on the Coat of Arms, but highlighted on page three, are the family motto and related crest – with the latter frequently different from the central motif.

Adding further variety to the rich cultural heritage that is represented by surnames is the appearance in recent times in lists of the most common names found throughout the United Kingdom of ones that include Khan, Patel and Singh – names that have proud roots in the vast sub-continent of India.

Echoes of a far distant past can still be found in our surnames and they can be borne with pride in commemoration of our forebears.

Chapter two:

The Horn of Leys

A name whose origin is not known with any degree of certainty, stretching back as it does through the dim mists of time and with a rather bewildering number of spelling variants, 'Burnett' nevertheless features prominently in Scotland's frequently turbulent historical record.

One theory is that it stems from the Old French 'burnette', or 'brunette', diminutives of 'brun' and indicating 'brown' or even 'dark brown', while some sources also suggest it may refer to a term for a type of woollen cloth that would have been dyed a dark brown.

However, rather than of Old French roots, other sources suggest it comes from the Old English surname 'Burnard', derived from the Anglo-Saxon 'Beornheard.'

This latter form of the name, along with the variant 'Bernard' and which would later assume the forms of 'Burnett' and 'Burnet', appear to have been adopted by those Anglo-Normans who began to settle in Scotland during the reign from 1124 to 1153 of King David I.

The king, who had been in English exile for a time in the royal court, had become enamoured with Norman customs, military and organisational skills and enterprise and, accordingly, held out the lure of settling in Scotland by offering them lands.

Among these ambitious and land-hungry Anglo-Normans was a family of Burnards/Bernards who settled in Roxburghshire, in the Borders.

It was this family that was destined to become the pre-eminent Burnetts of Leys, later known as the House of Burnett, in the northeast of Scotland.

In Roxburghshire, the family first held lands in the barony of Farningdoun: Roger Bernard of Farningdoun is recorded in 1200, while one of his sons, Ralph, is recorded in 1208 in the Episcopal Records of Glasgow as having provided the Church with peat, for fuel, to the Bishop of Glasgow as part of dues owed to the Church.

Nearly 45 years later, in 1252, another son, Richard Burnet, is on record as having sold part of the Farningdoun lands to Melrose Abbey, while other Borders and Lowlands offshoots of the original

Farningdoun family were the Burnets of Burnetland and Barns, in Peeblesshire and the Burnards of Ardross and Currie who held lands in Fife and Midlothian.

It was through Alexander Burnard that the Burnets of Farningdoun began their exodus from the Borders to the northeast.

A staunch supporter of the great warrior king Robert the Bruce during the War of Independence from 1296 to 1328 and following the king's victory over the English army of King Edward II at Bannockburn in 1314, he was rewarded for his loyalty nine years later by the grant of land on the banks of the River Dee, west of Aberdeen and appointed Royal Forester of the Forest of Drum.

His badge of office was a symbolic hunting horn and, known as the Horn of Leys this was later incorporated into the Burnett Coat of Arms and is on display to this day in their ancestral seat Crathes Castle.

The Horn of Leys, meanwhile, takes its name from the small, artificial island known as a crannog where they first took up residence on the Loch of Leys.

Held by the Burnetts of Leys for almost 400

years and now owned and managed along with its extensive grounds by the National Trust for Scotland, Crathes Castle was passed into the care of the trust in 1951 by Sir James Burnett, 13th Baronet of Leys, in order to preserve its important historical and architectural heritage.

A condition of the gift to the nation was that a room be reserved in Crathes Castle for the display of Burnett memorabilia, including the Horn of Leys, while the Burnett family of the chiefly line now live close to the castle in the House of Crathes.

Built on part of the land granted to the family in 1323, work on the castle's construction began in 1553 but was not completed until nearly 45 years later because of the turbulent politics of the time.

Open to visitors, the castle is home to a collection of portraits and its original Scottish renaissance painted ceilings in three of its Jacobean rooms – the Chamber of Nine Worthies, the Chamber of Muses and the Green Lady's Room.

For nature lovers, its 530 acre estate boasts woodlands and nearly four acres of walled garden.

Nearby is Muchalls Castle, work on which was completed in 1627 by Sir Thomas Burnett, 1st Baronet of Leys – more of whom later – and noted for its fine plasterwork ceilings; it passed out of the family's ownership in 1822.

Offshoots of the Burnets/Burnetts in the northeast of Scotland include the Burnetts of Kirkhill, of Camphill, Monboddo, Kemnay, Crimond and Craigmyle.

It was a son of the latter family, William Burnett of Craigour, Campbell and Tillihaire who was among the many Scots slain in the disastrous battle of Pinkie, fought on September 10, 1547, near Musselburgh, in East Lothian, when a 25,000-strong English army under the Duke of Somerset decisively defeated a 35,000-strong Scots army under the Earl of Arran.

Also known as the battle of Pinkie Cleugh, it was fought during the 'Rough Wooing', an attempt by England's dynastically ambitious Henry VIII to force upon the Scots agreement for the future marriage of his infant son Edward to the infant Mary, Queen of Scots.

Despite their superior numbers, what led to the defeat of the Scots in what became known as 'Black Saturday' was that Somerset was backed by a fleet of naval guns at the mouth of the River Esk, and the early loss in the battle of the Scots cavalry after it launched a premature and wild charge on the massed and disciplined English ranks.

In the following century, between 1638 and 1649, a bitter civil war raged between the forces of those Presbyterian Scots who had signed a National Covenant and those loyal to King Charles I of the Royal House of Stuart.

Described as 'the glorious marriage day of the kingdom with God', the Covenant renounced Catholic belief, pledged to uphold the Presbyterian religion, and called for free parliaments and assemblies.

Signed at Edinburgh's Greyfriars Church on February 28, 1638 by Scotland's nobles, barons,

burgesses and ministers, it was subscribed to the following day by hundreds of ordinary people, while copies were made and dispatched around Scotland and signed by thousands more.

Those who supported the Covenant were known as Covenanters, and one of their leading lights was Sir Thomas Burnett, 1st Baronet of Leys who, although his date of birth is not known, is recorded as having matriculated from Aberdeen University in 1603.

Having succeeded his father Alexander Burnett six years after matriculation, he was made an honorary burgess of Aberdeen in 1620, the same year in which he was knighted and raised to the peerage as a Baronet of Nova Scotia (New Scotland), the former Scottish colony in present-day New Brunswick, Canada.

An early supporter of the Covenant, he was a member of the powerful body known as the Tables, charged with enforcing its adherence at the point of a sword in areas that remained recalcitrant – particularly in Burnett's home turf of the northeast.

Opposing the Covenanters were Royalists such as James Graham, 1st Marquis of Montrose – ironically a kinsman of Burnett and who had originally supported the Covenanting cause – but the pair on occasion managed to forge mutually beneficial accommodations with one another.

During his great military campaigns against the Covenanters from 1644 to 1645, a year that became known as the Year of Miracles, Montrose enjoyed great success, but defeat came at the battle of Philiphaugh, near Selkirk, in August of 1645.

Escaping the field of battle and seeking foreign exile for a time, he returned to his native land to fight for Charles I's successor, Charles II, but defeated in battle he was executed in Edinburgh in 1650, while his kinsman Sir Thomas Burnett died three years later.

Over the years, the Burnetts of Burnetland and Barns had contended over the chieftainship of the family.

Matters were resolved amicably in 1993 when the title of the family was formally changed to the House of Burnett and, through the authority of Scotland's Lord Lyon King of Arms – responsible for all matters genealogical and heraldic relating to families and clans – James C.A. Burnett of Leys, Baron of Kilduthie, was recognised as Chief of the Name and Arms of Burnett.

Chapter three:

Fame and infamy

**Through endeavours and pursuits ranging from
the law and the Church to scholarship and the
battlefield, bearers of the Burnett/Burnet name
have gained distinction – while others notoriety.**

A brother of the Covenanting Sir Thomas
Burnett, Robert Burnet born in 1592, was admitted to
the Scottish Bar in 1617 and, as Lord Crimond, was a
Judge of the Court of Session.

He died in 1661, while one of his sons was
the theologian, historian and writer Gilbert Burnet,
Bishop of Salisbury.

Born in 1643, after studying at Marischal
College, Aberdeen, he was appointed professor of
divinity at Glasgow University in 1669. King's
chaplain for a time to King Charles II and appointed
Bishop of Salisbury in 1689, he died in 1715.

Another Burnett appointed to the Court of
Session was James Burnett, Lord Monboddo.

Born in 1714 in Howe of Mearns,
Aberdeenshire, and considered one of the greatest
intellects of his time, he was nevertheless ridiculed for

his theory – in advance of Charles Darwin – that humankind was descended from apes.

His title of Lord Monboddo, meanwhile, was based on his family seat, Monboddo House, in Howe of the Mearns, and now a magnificent category B listed building.

A genial host to the national bard Robert Burns when he visited his Edinburgh home, and author of a number of works including the six-volume *Of the Origin and Progress of Language*, he died in 1799.

Admitted to the Scottish bar in 1845, George Burnett was born in 1822 at Kemnay, Aberdeenshire.

An authority on all matters pertaining to Scottish heraldry and genealogy, he held the post of Scotland's Lord Lyon King of Arms from 1866 until his death in 1890.

On the battlefields of the terrible carnage of the First World War, Major-General Sir James Burnett of Leys, 13th Baronet of the name, was the distinguished and highly decorated soldier born at Crimond, Aberdeenshire, in 1880.

A colonel of the Gordon Highlanders and in command of a brigade on the Western Front, he was mentioned in despatches on no fewer than two occasions, awarded the Distinguished Service Order twice, made a member of France's Legion d'honneur and appointed a companion of the Order of the Bath.

He died in 1953, while it was two years before his death that he gifted Crathes Castle to the nation through the National Trust for Scotland.

In more contemporary times, Charles John Burnett is the distinguished Scottish antiquarian and former officer at arms born in the Burnett heartland of Aberdeenshire in 1940.

Educated at Gray's Art School, Aberdeen and Edinburgh University, he has worked for a number of museums including the National Museum of Antiquities, Edinburgh, and the Scottish United Services Museum at Edinburgh Castle.

Having served in posts that include Dingwall Pursuivant of Arms in Ordinary, Ross Herald of Arms in Ordinary, Ross Herald Extraordinary and a former president of the Heraldry Society of Scotland, he is also the author of *Crannog to Castle: A History of the Burnett Family in Scotland*.

From scholarship to decidedly less salubrious matters, one infamous twentieth century Scottish bearer of the Burnett name was the Aberdeen murderer

Henry John Burnett, who has the dubious distinction of being the last man to be hanged in Scotland – while his execution was the subject of controversy on the basis of his mental health at the time the crime was committed.

Born in Aberdeen in 1942, it was from July 23 to July 25, 1963 that he was tried and then found guilty at the High Court in Aberdeen for the murder of merchant seaman Thomas Guyan.

Guyan had married Margaret May in 1957 and the couple moved into a flat in the city's Jackson Terrace.

A son was born a year later, followed by a second in 1961 – but Guyan was not the father. This had led to marital problems and Margaret sought a divorce, but her husband refused.

In December of 1962 Margaret met Burnett, and their relationship blossomed to the extent that she left her husband and moved in with him, along with one of her young sons in May of 1963.

But Burnett doubted his paramour's fidelity, believing she would leave him, and took to locking her in every time he left the house. Upset by this state of affairs, when she met her estranged husband Thomas Guyan by chance, she moved back in with him.

This was on May 31, only a few short weeks after she had left him for Burnett, and later that day, along with her friend Georgina Cattanagh, she arrived back at Burnett's home in Skene Terrace to collect her son.

Burnett was heard to cry: "Margaret, Margaret, you are not going to leave me!" before holding a knife to her throat and closing the door.

Cattanagh kept pounding on the door until Burnett at last opened it and ran off in a state of distress down the street, leaving Margaret shaken but unharmed.

Events reached their bloody climax later that day when Burnett managed to obtain a shotgun and cartridges from his brother's house, and made his way to Jackson Terrace where Margaret, her son and friend had returned.

Forcing his way into the flat at gunpoint, he shot Guyan point-blank in the face as he emerged from the kitchen, leaving him dead on the floor.

Taking Margaret from the flat at gunpoint, Burnett dragged her down a lane to a nearby garage where he stole a car after threatening the owner with the shotgun, and then drove off leaving Margaret behind.

Pursued by police, he was finally apprehended near the town of Ellon by two police constables, having offered no resistance.

At his trial, his defence team – backed by the expert witness testimony of three distinguished psychiatrists – argued he should be reprieved on psychiatric grounds, having exhibited psychopathic tendencies in the past.

But this was dismissed by the Crown after the jury found him guilty of murder – on the basis that the argument for capital punishment hinged upon the use of a firearm, of which Burnett was clearly guilty.

A petition for a reprieve from execution from not only his own family but, unusually, also that of his victim was rejected.

Accordingly, on August 15, 1963, the 21-year-old Burnett was hanged at HM Prison, Craiginches, the last man to be hanged in Scotland.

Chapter four:

On the world stage

**Bearers of the Burnett name and its popular
spelling variant 'Burnet' have gained fame and
acclaim through a diverse and colourful range of
endeavours and pursuits.**

On the stage, **Carol Burnett** is the veteran
American comedian, actress, singer and writer born in
1933 in San Antonio, Texas.

Best known for her *Carol Burnett Show*,
which ran on television from 1967 to 1978, gathering
numerous awards including Emmys and Golden
Globes along the way, the show was the first of
its kind in America to be hosted by a woman and
featured song and dance routines, comedy sketches
and characters created by Burnett.

Much earlier, in 1959, she was the recipient
of a Tony Award nomination for her Broadway
performance in *Once Upon a Mattress* and another
nomination in 1995 for *Moon Over Buffalo*.

On the big screen, her credits include the
1974 *The Front Page* and, from 1982, *Annie*, while in
2005, recognised as "one of America's most cherished

entertainers", she was awarded the Presidential Medal of Freedom "for enhancing the lives of millions of Americans and her extraordinary contributions to American entertainment."

Behind the camera lens, **Alan Burnett** is the American television writer and producer best known for his animation work for Hannah-Barbera Productions, Walt Disney and Warner Bros.

Born in 1950, major productions he has been involved in include the *Scrooge McDuck* cartoon series and Disney's *Adventurers of the Gummi Bears*.

Also behind the camera lens, **Charles Burnett** is the American film producer, cinematographer and writer born in 1944 in Vicksburg, Mississippi.

Hailed by the *Chicago Times* as "one of America's very best filmmakers", his credits include the 1978 *Killer of Sheep*, the 1990 *To Sleep with Anger* and, from 2007, *Namibia: The Struggle for Liberation*.

On British shores and with the popular spelling variant 'Burnet', **Alistair Burnet** was the veteran journalist and broadcaster best known as the chief presenter of ITN's flagship television programme News at Ten.

More formally known as Sir James William Alexander Burnet after being awarded a knighthood in 1984 for services to journalism and broadcasting, he was born to Scottish parents in 1928 in Sheffield, Yorkshire.

A history graduate of Worcester College, Oxford, his first foray into journalism was as a reporter for the Scottish newspaper the *Glasgow Herald*, followed in 1958 with the *Economist*, where he was subsequently appointed associate editor.

Making the move to television in 1963, he became political editor of ITN and was its main anchor for coverage of the 1964, 1966 and 1970 General Elections.

Ever versatile, he was also the main anchor for coverage of the Apollo 11 Moon landing in 1969.

Having helped to launch *News at Ten* in 1967 and working as its main presenter on and off over the following decades until he made his final presentation in 1991, as a commentator he also covered major events including British and American elections and the wedding in 1981 of Lady Diana Spencer and Prince Charles.

The recipient of the BAFTA Richard

Dimbleby Award on a number of occasions, he died in 2012.

Born in Sheffield in 1924 and also on British television screens, **Hugh Burnett** was the producer who first joined BBC Radio in 1949, going on to present his *Personal Call* series – interviews with prominent international figures – later adapted for television.

As a television documentary maker he made a number of films in 1971 – often shot secretly – about apartheid.

These included *South Africa Loves Jesus* and *The Colour Line*, while on a much different tack, he also made a number of programmes about the supernatural and other mysteries – including the 1975 *The Ghost Hunters*, the 1976 *The Mystery of Loch Ness* and, a year later, *Out of This World*.

Also a talented cartoonist – with depictions of monks one of his specialities – his work appeared in magazines including the satirical *Private Eye*, the *Oldie* and the *New Statesman*; he died in 2011.

Born in Hulme, Manchester, in 1943, **Paul Burnett** is the veteran radio disc jockey who has worked for a number of radio stations including Radio Luxembourg and BBC Radio 1.

It was while working on Radio Luxembourg in the late 1960s that he made a rather unusual discovery.

This was a number of recordings of Nazi propaganda broadcasts during the Second World War recorded by the Irish-born William Joyce, better known to British listeners as 'Lord Haw-Haw', and broadcast from a number of Luxembourg stations at the time while the country was under German occupation.

On both radio and television, **Brian Burnett** is the Scottish presenter whose television shows for STV have included *Passport Quiz* and *Party Animals* and whose work for BBC Radio Scotland includes the music request show *Get It On*.

Back on American shores, **Erin Burnett** is the television news anchor who hosts CNN's *Erin Burnett OutFront*.

Born in 1976 in Mardela Springs, Maryland and having reported extensively from hotspots include Iran, Afghanistan and Yemen, she is a member of the Council on Foreign Relations.

An award-winning American photo-journalist, **David Burnett** was born in 1946 in Salt Lake City, Utah.

Beginning work as a freelance photographer for *Time* and *Life* magazines in 1968, covering events in America and also the Vietnam War, he later joined the French photo agency Gamma before co-founding his own agency, Contact Press Images.

Much of his work covering the Iranian revolution in 1979 was published by *Time*, including its 'Man of the Year' portrait of the Ayatollah Khomeini, while his many awards include the 1980 World Press Photo Award for his image of a distraught Cambodian woman holding her child in her arms as she waits for food to be distributed in a refugee camp.

In the highly competitive world of sport, **Jamie Burnett** is the Scottish former snooker player born in 1975 in Hamilton, South Lanarkshire who, for 20 consecutive years between 1996 and 2016 was ranked within the world's top 64 players.

On the cricket pitch, **Calvin Burnett**, born in Dundee in 1990, is the Scottish right-arm pace bowler whose first-class debut for his country was in 2013 against Australia A, while on the tennis court **Nastassja Burnett**, born in Rome in 1992 to a Polish mother and Scottish father, is the Italian Player who was ranked at No. 21 in the Women's Tennis Association (WTA) in 2014.

In the swimming pool, **Simon Burnett**, born in Oxford in 1983, is the swimmer who has held the British record in the 100 and 200 metre freestyles, while **Richard Burnett**, born in 1967 in Cwmparc, Rhonda and nicknamed 'Prince of Wales', is the Welsh professional darts player and former World No. 1 who won the 1995 Embassy World Darts Championship.

In the fast-paced game of ice hockey, **Garrett 'Rocky' Burnett**, born in 1975 in Coquitlam, British Columbia, is the Canadian former player who played for the Mighty Anaheim Ducks of the National Hockey League in the 2003-2004 season.

In the creative world of art and with the spelling variant 'Burnet', **John Burnet**, born in about 1784, was the Scottish painter and engraver who, after moving from Edinburgh to London in 1806, became a noted painter of landscapes and portraits.

As an engraver, his work was also much in demand – providing illustrations, for example, for editions of Sir Walter Scott's *Waverley* novels and the poems of Robert Burns; a Fellow of the Royal Society, he died in 1868.

Again with the spelling variant 'Burnet', the legacy of the accomplished eighteenth century

Scottish architect **John Burnet** survives to this day in the form of a number of noted Glasgow buildings.

Born in 1814 and executing his architectural designs in Glasgow, he was largely self-taught and employed an eclectic range of styles including Italianate, Scottish Baronial, Gothic and Renaissance, while works which survive include the Glasgow Stock Exchange in what is now Nelson Mandela Place.

Taking up his architect's mantle, his son **Sir John James Burnet** was born in Glasgow in 1857.

Important commissions undertaken by him include the Cenotaph in Glasgow's George Square, completed in 1924, and the city's Charing Cross Mansions, completed in 1891.

Also responsible for Selfridges Department Store in London, completed in 1919, and a founder member of the Royal Incorporation of Architects in Scotland, he was knighted in 1914 for his work on the Edward VII Galleries in the British Museum; he died in 1938.

From architecture to the world of music, **Joseph Henry 'T Bone' Burnett III** is the American musician, songwriter and record producer who was a guitarist in Bob Dylan's band during the 1970s.

Born in 1948 in St Louis, Missouri, his work on film music has netted him a number of Grammy Awards including for the 2004 *Cold Mountain* and the 2006 *Walk the Line*.

In the world of the written word, **Frances Hodgson Burnett**, born in Cheetham, Manchester in 1849, was the British-American children's novelist and playwright whose famous books are her 1885 *Little Lord Fauntleroy*, the 1905 *A Little Princess* and, from 1911, *The Secret Garden*; she died in 1924.

In a much different writing genre, **William Riley Burnett**, also known as W.R. Burnett, was the American novelist and screenwriter born in 1899 in Springfield, Ohio, best known for his 1929 crime novel *Little Caesar*.

Adapted for film in 1931 and starring a then relatively unknown Edward G. Robinson, the film is now regarded as a screen classic; following *Little Caesar* with his 1932 *Scarface*, Burnett died in 1982.